Cancer, Be Not Proud

Jim Wilson

Contents

*This book is dedicated to my wife of 45 years, Mimi Lord,
who undoubtedly is the main reason I am still alive as this book is
being prepared for publication. She has addressed my every known
need and has anticipated countless others.
We're more in love than ever before.*

Introduction

On August 28, 2022, cancer shattered my world—perceptually, physically, and emotionally—as well as my existing hope of enjoying a long, comfortable retirement. Suddenly, my muscles turned into overcooked pasta; I started to spin around and was about to collapse when my wife caught me and steered me to a sofa, saving me as she has done many times since.

Even though I had taken reasonably good care of myself, cancer had other plans. It hurled me into a new world of medical procedures, kindness from strangers, and unfamiliar variations of exhaustion and brain fog. My type of cancer, glioblastoma, is notoriously dangerous; I am painfully aware of its speed and tenacity.

This book is something of a diary of an older couple's refusal to capitulate. I explore and describe a list of "good habits," which used to be called "virtues" in better, less-divisive days. Writing the enclosed chapters not only proved to be a worthwhile intellectual challenge, but also created an online venue where numerous people provided us with encouragement and insights. Indeed, our readers became another prop for survival.

We hope that you will find our encounter with the Grim Triumvirate—old age, disease, and death—helpful, perhaps even inspirational. Maybe you'll find a few tools and perspectives for weathering the inevitable stormy seas. Because we are trying to avoid the perils of existential despair and/or religious fanaticism, there will not be any easy solutions. Yet we have been able to hold the cancer at bay (so far) and have been gratified by so much kindness, support, and medical skill.

The Grim Triumvirate will never depart from any of our lives, but it provides surprising opportunities for creating a greater community and a growing sense of dignified decency.

September 1, 2023

Chapter 1

Opening Salvos

November 1, 2022

To paraphrase Dickens, this has been the best of times and the worst of times. On August 28, 2022, my wife, Mimi, took me to Tampa General Hospital's Emergency Room because I had collapsed to a couch. Because there was a large, fast-growing cancer in my brain, doctors needed to operate as soon as possible, on August 30. It turned out to be an extremely aggressive form of cancer, glioblastoma.

The first good news was that the surgeons, Dr. Vakharia and Dr. Peto, brilliantly removed a 1.3-pound tumor without doing any observable damage to my cognition. Obviously, there is the other good news that I am still alive.

We immediately adopted a cluster of good habits. Fortunately, my radiation oncologist has been thrilled by my progress: very few headaches are a symptom of brain health. He also thought that my condition improved twice as much as expected.

The interesting, potential good news is that there may be a causal link between those good habits and the recent positive outcomes. Presently, this hypothesis has not been scientifically verified. But practicing these habits provided us with some autonomy and hope. May some of these habits prove to be beneficial to us and others.

For anyone so inclined, this newsletter will provide myriad reflections on the continuing ordeal. This will not always be comforting reading; I have been abiding too long in the shadow of the Valley of Death. But, where there is death, there is life. Where there is life, there is love and kindness.

Overall, my interactions with friends, family, healthcare providers, neighbors and others led to the following conclusion that I could never have imagined. My cancer experience— including the terrifying diagnosis, extensive brain surgery, and ongoing treatments—has been one of the most inspiring periods of my life, restoring a great deal of faith in human nature during these increasingly fractious times.

Chapter 2

Bucket List

November 6, 2022

Cancer patients fearing a daunting future often create their "bucket lists." I used to like the term "bucket list" because it was a rare example of American humor about death:

"Make a list of all the things you want to do or acquire before you 'kick the bucket.'"

However, my previous attempts to create a bucket list sometimes raised unsatisfying questions: "What should I get? Where to go? Got enough money? Do I really have to do that item on the list?" And so forth. The bucket list seemed too American—all about you and your unfulfilled desires.

Well, an alternative to the traditional bucket list suddenly plopped into my awareness: *"Everything* is on the bucket list." I'll share some recent experiences with my new, evolving bucket list.

I was contemplating our jacaranda tree while sitting on our front porch. This ancient being was becoming spindlier every year. Then, fortunately, Florida became awash with rain. And the tree has become almost bloated with vitality while its fern-like leaves flutter away. May the ground in time become covered with the jacaranda's purple flowers.

To watch the tree strengthen and walk amongst the petals turns out to have been on my bucket list—I just didn't know it.

I'm constantly finding other situations that weren't on my previous bucket list. For example, every time I interact with a relative or friend it opens new perspectives and reflections; every personal relationship has its unique transitory beauty. Restarting my newsletter and hearing from readers that it meant something important to them gives me joy. Enjoying a cloud, a bird, a sunrise over the Bay—all join the list. A bucket list like this becomes a continuing celebration of one's life moments, perpetually changing in the sunlit sky.

However, as I contemplate my bucket list further, I realize that the statement, "Everything is on the bucket list," is too universal and that I had gone overboard. It could be interpreted that every situation is something you wished for, and thus it does not comport with common sense.

There are lots of things I wish had never happened. I never wanted to be diagnosed with cancer; I never wanted our wonderful dog to die after her recent surgery. However, being in the moment helps to open one up to compassionate acceptance. It resembles the famous Zen saying, "Every situation is the guru."

Of course, you may prefer to keep your existing bucket list, which may have already given you excitement and gratification. It is hard to refute the adage: "Eat, drink and be merry, for tomorrow you may die." Or perhaps one version of the bucket list will be useful to you at certain times, and another version at other times.

If some of your plans run astray, don't be too hard on yourself. I remember my darkest days surrounding surgery and treatments. If you were to ask me then whether being able to finish sentences was on my bucket list, I would have jumped at the offer. Now, I am deep with gratitude at being able to compose and share these thoughts with you.

So, you need not worry about universal abstractions— simply contemplate your newest situation and your evolving goal of embracing life itself, even its inevitable pain and suffering. Gratefully accept whatever addresses some of your deepest desires. You may have fewer frustrations, such as "too little, too late," that stemmed from your previous bucket list. And you no longer need to keep the old list in your memory, which is a hassle in and of itself.

On a recent day, I said goodbye to a close friend who had flown in to visit me. As he left the car, I rolled down the window and shouted, "You're on my bucket list." He appeared to wipe a tear. I then joked, "Don't worry, I'm on your bucket list too." This alleviation of responsibilities made him burst out laughing. And I realized that the act of telling others that they're on my bucket list (in other words, that I deeply care about them) is very high on my bucket list.

Chapter 3

Methylated!!

November 13, 2022

"Methylated?" I didn't know what that meant either. Turns out to be among the sweetest words I'd ever heard since my wife, Mimi, and I exchanged wedding vows many years ago.

We recently went for a regular consult with our oncologist at Tampa General Hospital. Every time we go, I am frightened that something terrible might be revealed. But we were about to be dealt a card of good fortune.

Just to be clear, my short-term memory has been impaired at times due to the cancer, so your narrator is less reliable than usual. Nor am I a medical expert, so don't take my medical descriptions too seriously. I haven't studied my disease very closely because I already knew that the future looked perilous.

Mimi brought to the appointment a printed copy of the Caris report, which had just been posted on my patient portal. The Caris report provides an analysis of the molecular profile of cancer cells that were removed during surgery and kept frozen until recently. When the radiation oncologist reviewed the report, he beamed, "Methylated!"

He said this is great news: the chemotherapy I've been taking is quite effective in fighting my form of cancer, cutting my mortality rate in half! If the cells had not been methylated, the outlook would have been more dismal and other treatments could be required.

With a friendly nod toward Mimi, the oncologist also said that my family's support is a major contribution to my well- being. And to the delight of his physician assistants, he applauded the fine medical team. After a round of high- fives, the doctor recommended that we go out and celebrate. We took this as "doctor's order."

I went to the outdoor bench to wait for Mimi to bring the car. The view was the same as I'd seen many times, both before radiation and afterward as I sat there reeling from its effects. But on that glorious day, the whole scene looked radically different, drenched in hope, optimism, and enthusiasm. I was also in a bit of shock, as surprised by this good fortune as I had been surprised by the original cancer diagnosis.

Sure, I'd had some alleviating fantasies about positive prognoses that provided short-term relief. This time, however, a surge of vitality permeated my mind, body, soul and perception—while my fantasies faded away. Reality had easily surpassed fantasy.

We drove to a Bayside restaurant to celebrate and were seated at water's edge facing a green burst of mangroves.

A gorgeous day. The sun-sparkled water was gracefully eased aside by a manatee, leaving silver slivers of water over its body and into its wake. We began with an agreed- upon toast: "Eat Well, Drink Well, For Tomorrow You May *Live*."

Suddenly, something ominous arose in my stream of consciousness, supporting the Buddha's admonition that good news can be as challenging as bad news: my hope and optimism may have gone a bit overboard. Sensing an opening, a "little voice" emerged, determined to convince me to soften some austere habits. This force can sometimes be benign, but it also can be raucous, ravenous, relentless, and potentially fatal—a dangerous combination of the voracious Shark in the movie Jaws and the Serpent in the Garden of Eden.

Richard Pryor brilliantly analyzed the "little voice" in a classic comedic performance; he described his drug addiction that led him to accidentally set himself on fire while freebasing cocaine. Pryor's little voice was constantly coming up with new arguments and temptations to coax him into maintaining his addiction.

In my situation, I had vigorously maintained a strict rule against eating sugar and all processed sweeteners, the development of which I'll describe in a future post on "Diet." I'd heard that cancer cells love sugar, boosting the tumor's growth. My will to live was so terrified that it wanted to take strict measures that might increase my perilously low survival rate.

As we joyfully sat at the waterside table, reflecting upon this sudden burst of good fortune, the will became less frightened. That little voice started clamoring for sugar:

"Let's celebrate by getting some delicious vegan ice cream—it even has berries! And why don't we pick up a dozen Bundt cakes to share with friends and neighbors? There's no need to keep asking the waitress if there is any sugar in each dish. This is an exceptionally good day, so let's get some frozen yoghurt and carrot cake!"

In the vignette above, I introduced the notion of awareness, which will play a major role in this newsletter; I hope to write a long essay/book on the benefits of increasing one's self-awareness. Thanks to Richard Pryor, I had already learned to spot the dangerous little voice and could take appropriate action. Although my greedy little voice continues to yammer away, I still haven't eaten any sugar.

In closing, I'd like to mimic the doctor's kind words about primary caregivers—often little-known people who sacrifice time, effort, and even money to help their suffering friends and relatives get through the day. May we all be safe, well, happy, and live with ease.

Chapter 4

"It All Ends"

November 19, 2022

While Mimi and I couldn't resist sharing the recent good news about the methylated cells, the cancer narrative of this newsletter presently runs the risk of becoming jumbled. We must back up a bit. The first newsletter raised two questions. First, how and why did the cancer diagnosis, long hospital stay, and subsequent events dramatically change my awareness and perceptions, leading to greater regard and hope for our fellow species? Second, what are the "good" habits that I am maintaining (all of which may continue to be beneficial and must be explained in more detail)?

 So, we are backing up to the initial part of this experience when we arrived in the Emergency Room, soon after Mimi helped me avert a collapse at home. Along the way, we shall see that this tumultuous ordeal has provided several "opportunities for transformation."

Tampa General Hospital's Emergency Room was different than any I had previously visited. The main waiting room resembled a vast automobile showroom, whose lack of flare was mitigated by tall surrounding windows revealing sunlight, clouds, trees, and a few welcome glances at Tampa Bay.

One of the most delightful interactions of kindness arose when someone offered warm blankets to Mimi and me as we stared blankly at the blue water, awaiting whatever was in store. That act of kindness was as comforting as the blanket itself. Little did I know how many warm blankets and warm memories were to come.

I was next directed to the intake room. A pleasant young woman began to discuss my condition. She didn't mention "stroke," so maybe this hospital visit was not going to be a big deal! But, of course, my recent collapses still indicated something was wrong. I lamented to her: "I'm within a week of my 75th birthday. I never had a major illness, and never needed many prescription drugs, but it looks like I'm not making it to 75 unscathed." Lifting sad eyes towards me, she observed, "It All Ends."

A staff member appeared and happily gave me a free aluminum walker. My thanks did not cover up internal horror: "What? I don't need that! Those walkers are noisy and clumsy, accoutrements of disease and old age."

Now, some readers might think the intake worker was too candid by mentioning The Concept-That-Shall-Not-Be-Named: Death. I felt some sympathy for her. She would have encountered numerous vegan jazzercise instructors, triathletes, and other new patients, reeling in their shock. So much denial. I had harbored my own version of denial by previously expecting to live to at least 95; my mother had lived to 103 and other relatives on her side survived well into their nineties. I had a history of good health, bolstered by beneficial habits and a spirit buoyed by an insatiable curiosity.

I remain grateful to the young intake worker. After all, she was restating The Buddha's Noble Truth that "everything changes." The steady influx of bad news had barely begun, yet my panicked intellect was already rushing around in my memory to discover the best course of action. It could not hide behind much denial.

I saw Mimi standing alone in the vast waiting room, staring at our crumbling world, and I headed there awkwardly with my new walker. Have you seen elderly couples huddled together, like two Hobbits trying to evade Sauron's Black Riders in *The Lord of the Rings*? We could barely exchange words, reluctant to exacerbate our growing alarm.

This admittedly bleak scene was fortunately interrupted by two rays of light. Two middle-aged women, one black and one white, carefully came towards us with concerned brows, increasing our alarm. They might have been social workers or nurses. With experienced kindness and patience, they shared two pieces of advice to an anxious couple that had never faced such a challenge. We shall explore their advice more deeply in a later newsletter.

Over the past weeks, I have frequently encountered nurses and other staff who remind me of Old Charon, the mythic Greek boatsman who steers souls down the River Styx towards an uncertain future. I particularly recall an elegant gentleman who escorted me to the radiation treatments, often with a mere touch or smile. These gentle beings provide comfort and reassurance while we passengers attempt to adapt. They have seen many shocked and suffering people, yet continue to help alleviate their loneliness.

Chapter 5

Two Women

November 22, 2022

As mentioned in the prior newsletter, two women approached us in the ER. I can't recall the exact moment when I got the brain cancer diagnosis, but their concern indicated a long haul ahead, whatever the diagnosis. The possibility of brain cancer had crossed my mind, and there would soon be consultations about major surgery to remove at least the bulk of the life-threatening and fast-growing tumor(s).

One of the women said she had a suggestion that might help: "Cautious optimism." This sounds about right, resembling, *Hope but No Expectations.* Hope and optimism are often in short supply, yet they are words of goodwill towards humanity and other life forms.

Still, the concept of "optimism" seems a bit problematic, beyond just any sugarcoating. I originally formulated and adopted the title of my newsletter, *Hope but No Expectations,* to limit the influences of optimism and pessimism. Pessimism is a risky perspective for someone who has wrestled with depression and occasional bouts of misanthropy. Both optimism and pessimism are presumptuous. They suggest considerable control over outcomes and remarkable foresight: things *will* get better, or things *will* get worse. I am not reassured, for instance, when someone tells me, "Everything is going to be alright." Having little or no idea about future developments, I prefer "fatalism," a partial, often reluctant, acceptance of whatever arises.

The philosopher Karl Popper warned that many ideologists get distorted by "historicism," thinking they can forecast the future. Marx and Hegel, for example, were so committed to their imaginary future that they tended to purge those who did not fulfill or agree with their predictions. The optimist seems vulnerable to too much bad news, while the pessimist may lose commitment even though life may be improving dramatically.

Indeed, the primary target of *Hope but No Expectations* is fighting pessimism more than optimism. Best to dismiss most pessimistic thoughts, while remaining wary of optimism. I pay little attention to thoughts of dying from cancer because I have no clear expectations about my future. And while I maintain hope, I put optimistic thoughts on the back burner.

I next turned to the other woman and asked for *her* advice regarding my situation. Without hesitation, she said, "Will" I was thunderstruck. Will? Will? Over the past several months, the concept of "will" had become a growing component of my lengthy project on exploring awareness. The working title of that project, still in progress, is: *A Map of Awareness, Subject to Revision.* Someday, I hope to share this.

So, what is will? I excitedly asked her. She did not hesitate: "Will, infused with love."

The women's two slogans have been boxing gloves in my fight against cancer. A dose of sustained hope and kindness in combination with a desire to embrace the rest of one's life.

I never saw them again. They probably will never read this newsletter, but they have helped me through these arduous times. So, thanks! May I remember to thank them during my upcoming Thanksgiving dinner with my family, a source of my greatest gratitude and strength.

Chapter 6

Topsy Turvy
December 2, 2022

One of the problems with major brain surgery is that you have much less of an idea of what is going on than before. It is hard to determine what causes the omnipresent fatigue and light-headed disorientation. Did they arise from cancer, surgery and anesthesiology, protracted hospitalization, radiation, side effects of chemotherapy and other drugs, periodic insomnia?

My visual world reveals significant brain damage. There remains a blind spot on the left side, which sometimes resembles a bad Cubist painting. There are even mild, periodic hallucinations—images the mind/brain pastes on my visual field like photographs.

In the hospital, I had to be assisted getting off the bed to my walker so that my wobbly bulk wouldn't pull someone down, injuring us both. Searching for a mutual chuckle, I told helpers that my mind seemed like the Magic Eight Ball; after posing a question, you pick up and shake the ball, and then stare at the cloudy image until you can make out the words. More than once, the Eight Ball could have stated, "Reply is hazy. Try again." My perceptual and cognitive world was clearly suffering from brain fog, making it almost impossible to read and to process fast-moving visual information.

My radiation oncologist had predicted that there would be significant improvement in vitality as the radiation, chemo, and other effects wore off. Fortunately, he was right. Almost every day, there seems to be a bit more stamina in the tank (periodic cardiovascular work has helped too). My sense of well-being was greatly enhanced by our children's visit for Thanksgiving. And this welcome change enables me to compare recent improvements with past and present difficulties.

As I sat at my desk recently, I was delighted that I felt much like my old self, and I realized that I had been partially disconnected from my "identity." I perceived a growing connection between my current and past selves, as if dominoes were lining up between the two. Then I felt a surge of vitality trickling through those identities, uniting them into a whole. Settling further into the chair, a similar line of dominoes connected my identities into the future, ending with darkness and mystery.

More abstractly, this experience may have provided an insight to the meaning of "identity," which is often commingled with the "will." It is hard to have an identity without a will, and vice versa. And, as noted, these perceptions suggest that identity is intimately tied with memory and imagination. After all the linkages had been made, I felt a little disappointed. A lot of previous neurotic problems jumped in: "You are still you, and you are still part of this troubled world." Nevertheless, I was grateful that more of me was back.

Two days ago, it was time for a milestone consultation with the neuro oncologist, Dr. Ranjan, to discuss my recent MRI. Alas, my emotional domain remains unstable. The day before the consult, the doctor called my wife Mimi to find out if I'd been taking any blood thinners, which I had not. This inquiry generated a fear that I might need another operation to remove new tumors. It was a rough night.

At the following morning appointment, Dr. Ranjan lucidly guided us through the MRI pictures on the screen. The Good News was the apparent absence of new cancer cells. The Bad News was a notable blood clot on one side of my brain, which will require frequent CT scans and potential draining. One of the images, however, resembled a full cauliflower pattern without any signs of fraying or other anomalies. I delightedly said, "It looks like an old-school brain." The doctor crisply replied, "It *is* an old-school brain— yet one that needs close monitoring."

This description of my topsy-turvy condition has encouraged me to stop when I encounter another beleaguered patient. I hope to gently take them by the hand and simply say, "Hi. I am Jim. I hope you will be feeling much better soon." Once again, we witness the Buddhist emotional alchemy of transmuting suffering into compassion. May we all feel better soon.

Chapter 7

Chicken Little

December 6, 2022

The prior newsletter described my recent surge in vitality and identity. Yet the drawback of rapid improvement during these lengthy struggles with serious illness is that one has more to lose. As Janis Joplin sang, "Freedom's just another word for nothing left to lose." During the initial stages, I had let go of a lot, all but forgetting the life that had transpired before we ventured into the ER.

After enduring the first round of chemo and radiation, I began to regain a sense of well-being, which, perhaps inevitably, was accompanied by growing anxiety about losing what I had gained. The fear of new cancer cells ballooned as we approached the recent doctor appointment, a fear that, thankfully, has not materialized so far. But now we must contend with the recently diagnosed blood clot. Two lethal threats instead of one.

A more pervasive fear emerged, which I have since named, "Chicken Little." Squawking something about the Sky, the bird barged into my meditative mind space, often called, "Home."

I never liked the name "Chicken Little." Why would the Little family name their offspring "Chicken," particularly when it was already a chicken? Furthermore, Chicken Little joined The Boy Who Cried Wolf, Cassandra, and other discredited doomsayers. Despite my wariness of pessimism, I have retained an interest in the apocalyptic aesthetic; *Doctor Strangelove* and Orwell's *1984* remain pivotal influences. More recently, I was deeply moved by the television series, *Station Eleven*.

Like fear, Chicken Little can be unbelievably annoying, even domineering— shrieking, darting about, scratching the floor. It was easy to confirm the resurgence of fear: constricted chest, shortness of breath, swirliness, and the discrete mental pain that grew as fear increased its domain.

Pema Chodron is the Buddhist nun who has frequently guided me through emotional minefields. She often advised that we need to face our emotional problems instead of avoiding them. This technique has generally served me well.

But letting Chicken Little into my mental home backfired; its frenetic energy created a dark hole in my abdomen, spreading its venom everywhere.

Still trying to work through this difficulty, I had an anxious morning in bed. When I used my walker to get to the bathroom, my knees unexpectedly buckled—my gait was the wobbliest in months. Mimi helped me stumble to a breakfast chair. For fear begets fear, and fear increases wobbliness and dizziness, which in turn creates more fear, and so on—particularly now that a fall could be catastrophic (compounded by a possibly dislodged blood clot).

This downward spiral really pissed me off. Time to bring in my inner warrior (more on this in later newsletters). I instructed the warrior, "Time for some chicken wings." The warrior nodded and started pursuing the chicken. I could hear them stomping and scratching around as the warrior could not catch the elusive, frantic bird. Its terrified squawks aggravated the situation.

There was a crash as the warrior fell. I inquired, "Are you alright?" Slowly picking her/himself up like a cat trying to compose itself after falling off a ledge, the warrior haughtily replied, "I slipped in a fetid pile of what is aptly called 'chicken-shit.'" We laughed.

Well, we couldn't find Chicken Little right away. Instead, we fortified our home to keep the damn thing away. However, the "will" admonished us not to get too eager to purge fear, lest the will could lose its power to regulate unruly appetites. The chicken was bound to return, anyway.

Now, you might not like this scatological or gastronomically incorrect (What? Chicken Wings!?) humor during such somber proceedings. One of the side effects of my increased vitality and identity is more raucous irreverence.

Chapter 8

"Maintain a Good Attitude"

December 16, 2022

We cancer victims receive lots of advice. Indeed, this newsletter is stuffed with advice, including advice on how to assess advice. The two recommendations I've heard the most are: "Day by day" and "Maintain a good attitude." Are these sayings Hallmarkey Malarkey, or is your narrator simply being a Grinch (particularly unwelcome during the holiday season)?

Of the two, I prefer "Day by day," which suggests a mixture of stoicism and determination to face uncertain odds. This perspective is particularly helpful through the daily grind of my second round of chemotherapy. There are the physical, drug-related side effects of exhaustion, wooziness, and severe constipation. In addition, the adverse psychological effects have become more pronounced, especially since we face up to six months or more of chemo treatments. "Day by day" is a truism, reminding us of ongoing challenges and joys. It is a staple among baseball players as they weather the fluctuations of their long season.

"Maintain a good attitude," on the other hand, sticks in my craw. It provides comfort to some; why question its validity? Upon cross-examination of my motives and beliefs, I recognized that this skepticism toward conventional wisdom and dogma is deeply embedded. As a lawyer, I could better interpret and apply the law's generalities to specific situations by perceiving the social norms and interests that animate much of the caselaw, legalistic arguments, and outcomes.

My previous work on America's political/legal economy was primarily based upon "Show Me the Money." The current inquiry takes more of a Buddhist-Existentialist perspective, trying to determine how much the widespread, understandable fear of death and decay permeates and distorts our conversations during these intense periods of our lives. How and why do we (or don't we) talk to each other about aging, sickness, dying, and death? Why does society assume that people caused their own illness and death?

I have always been suspicious of "Blame the Victim" or "The Victim is not Responsible" arguments. Here, cutting off the chain of causation before death or survival raises a huge question: What caused this global plague of cancer in the first place? Isn't it likely that ubiquitous chemical pollutants and excessive stress are more responsible than attitudes?

Let's parse the phrase word by word. "Maintain" not only seems a bit bossy, but it also sounds like, "Put on a Happy Face!" In addition, it implies that you can preserve a fixed attitude for quite some time. Unfortunately, sadness is one of the side effects of my current drug cocktail. And now that I've progressed beyond surgery and radiation to a bit more normalcy, neurotic thoughts have surged as I fear setbacks. Moods are cyclical, always have been. So, should I be self-critical for acknowledging and analyzing these thoughts and emotions? Should I take Pema Chodron's advice again and openly contemplate my weaknesses—is that a bad attitude?

Moving on to the second word of the phrase: "a." Why is there only "a" good attitude? Perhaps there are a variety of useful attitudes, appropriate for various situations. The article "a" suggests there is a single "right answer." Currently, I am inclined to substitute: "Develop an *open* attitude," which can recruit curiosity and wonder to encounter whatever may arise, day by day. One needs flexibility rather than a single, idealized version of a positive attitude.

Of course, one mustn't totally reject "good attitude," even if it is far from clear what the adviser is recommending. Who can argue against something "good?" But good for what? Perhaps I have overreacted to the phrase; the aphorism may be relevant and possibly a useful tool for some. At a minimum, it implies that one shouldn't spend too much time with a "bad attitude."

When waiting one day at the hospital after radiation, I sat next to an elderly person who was complaining about everything: the heat, the delays, the uncomfortable bench. As she went on and on, apparently a habit, I thought how tiring it must be to put up with all that frustration while trying to combat cancer. On the other hand, sometimes a "bad attitude" may be helpful. You may need to abide in some of your fear and suffering, lest you suppress it while it continues to gnaw at your soul. Equally important, you are going to need a bad/fierce attitude to fight cancer.

Doubts about the positive-attitude phrase escalated when a couple of friends, attempting to encourage and compliment me, stated that my recent improvement was attributable to my "good attitude." These well-intentioned comments triggered a deeper irritation that revealed some of America's cultural norms about life, death and dying.

We are encountering the "just world" belief: we all have a desire to see more fairness, implying that people should get what they deserve. This suggests that the patient is at fault for having an insufficient attitude. Imagine that the results from my treatments had been poor: "Too bad about your diagnosis of terminal brain cancer. Must have been your bad attitude." Susan Sontag wrote in *Illness as Metaphor* that we tend to see someone's ailments as a commentary on their character. Why?

A good-attitude goal is likely to be unachievable anyway, thus causing more guilt, frustration, and fear. When I asked a close friend, who is suffering from a different long-term illness, how she responds when someone remarks on her "good attitude," she saucily replied, "Easy for *you* to say."

The collective and individual consciousness seeks more control over our perilous existence. Perhaps living life is always an art form, trying to balance (even harmonize) our determination and belief structure against our willingness to accept an uncertain and seemingly random future. Forced optimism is likely to be more beneficial than wallowing in despair, but we must be careful when selecting appropriate attitudes and techniques. The truth is that we all would like the mind to be the dominant force which can prevail over matter (in this case, cancer). Alas, the other truth is that the mind does not always succeed.

Chapter 9

Some Disclaimers

December 23, 2022

So far, this newsletter has aspired to clearly describe the states of mind of a patient engaged in a protracted war with cancer, hopefully providing some comfort to fellow sufferers ("You are not alone") and greater understanding for those who are in contact with them. Our previous letters examined some of the American sloganeering about death and dying, an uncertain process that reveals the pitfalls of veering towards the extremes of thoughts and emotions. But we are about to make a notable transition away from abiding primarily within the journey. The letters will become more didactic, recommending "good habits." So, it might be helpful to get some disclaimers out of the way.

1. I am not a certified expert in any field, aside from law. Nor do I relentlessly pursue medical journals or *YouTube* on wellness or physical therapy. The main advantage to my readers is that I will never be pushing supplements!

2. This approach to habits, which I believe has been remarkably successful in constraining my brain cancer, *may or may not have been* the primary reason for my ongoing recovery. My case is "anecdotal," the statisticians' polite euphemism for "statistically insignificant." Indeed, one of the longer-term goals of this newsletter is to encourage the government and the healthcare industry to investigate more deeply some possible causal linkages. If processed sugar is nearly as harmful as cigarettes, why aren't there more studies and disclosures about its risks?

   Of course, there are always counterarguments. I was quite diligent about "good habits" before getting brain cancer. So, if the healthy habits didn't protect me before, why should I think they're helping me now? Or, instead, what would have happened in the hospital if I had *not* taken pretty good care of myself previously?

3. When I first embarked on the written sayings of the Buddha to better understand my evolving meditation practice, I read his caution to followers: don't follow my techniques and theories with blind faith, degrading them into rigid dogma. Pursue the path for some time, and then *verify for yourself* the efficacy. This pragmatic, empirical approach enabled me to gain further trust in the Buddha.

4. As I mentioned in a previous newsletter, there is a tendency among some to "blame the victim." Most of us have tried to maintain some good habits but inevitably go off course at times. We are all stuck on the wheel of fortune, so let's continue to develop more sympathy for our fellow beings who are struggling to remain alive with some sense of dignity. Perhaps we've reached the time to discuss the importance of adopting more self-forgiveness, the first step towards developing compassion for yourself. But we'll save that inquiry for a future newsletter.

5. Nor do we need to create a whole set of gerontological "correct" or "incorrect" phrases. Ailing patients are bound to be—at least some of the time—bitter, lonely, and frightened, as well as jealous of other people's health. If everything becomes a linguistic mine-field, fiercely enforced with dogmatic prohibitions, real conversation will be diminished. As Melvyn Douglas sadly observed in the great movie, *Being There:* "Nobody wants to talk to a dying old man." Also, who wants to talk to any jaundiced geezer who smugly judges every noun, adjective, and concept for "violations;" jumps to condemnation; and ascribes vile motives to those who disagree or transgress?

It would be tragic to create even more barriers to open and honest relationships. Having said that, I did stumble across one word that seems quite offensive. While staring out the window, I reflected on my inability to get out of the house much, with most outdoor ventures consisting of trips to doctor appointments, blood tests, and brain scans. I realized I'm becoming an invalid. Wait a second: "Invalid?!" "I am "in**val**id?"—lacking all validity? Sounds like the Third Reich.

Chapter 10

Escaping the Doldrums

January 4, 2023

Sigh. Back in the doldrums.

While I remain perpetually grateful to the wag who dubbed the term, "drug cocktail," one elusive question is the nature of constantly changing side effects, or of something far worse. Recently, my left foot would quiver, keeping me awake at night. My doctor diagnosed seizure activity, doubled the anti-seizure medicine, and put me on alert for possible headaches or other major disruptions due to the blood clot. So far, the medication seems to be working, and the tremors have subsided significantly. There will be ongoing MRI's and CT scans to monitor both the cancer and the subdural hematoma.

Not surprisingly, this new existential threat of a seizure-related fall added to a growing sense of malaise. My earlier senses of fear, novelty, and determination were being undermined by fatigue and self-pity. To paraphrase two musical philosophers, Robert Plant and Jimmy Page of Led Zeppelin: "Good Times, Bad Times, [We've] All Had Our Share."

So, how to snap out of this dreary fog and take advantage of the "opportunity for transformation" that arises whenever the fear of mortality surges? I need to recommit to the worthwhile core attitudes, habits, and viewpoints that reinforce each other in a virtuous circle. Furthermore, I would like to improve myself to attain a somewhat more joyful identity than before, with an outlook of enhanced awareness, kindness, and gratitude.

Right now, the numerous good habits (diet, exercise, meditation, friendships, etc.) all seem to point in the same direction, but there is no clear destination. Based on my legal experience, I have turned to an intellectual technique to sort through numerous, often conflicting, directives and advice. Influenced by Aristotle and Wittgenstein, I utilize the notion of "purpose" to try to figure out the meaning and utility of various directives, as well as the tools to approach those objectives.

The next step is to sequence one's purposes/goals. Which ones are short, intermediate, or long-term? Identifying the short-term goal is easy: defeat cancer, and even sneer at it should it permanently leave me alone. A major intermediate aspiration is to write this newsletter so it might continue to benefit myself and many others. The third goal is more ambitious, perhaps venturing into the risky, divisive ground of the "religious." What enduring point of view could help produce the type of personality we wish to grow into for the next few decades?

I have spent months pondering this third goal and trying to come up with the right phrase to capture its essence. First, it seemed necessary to address a common critique of Buddhism that I encountered in college. Critics have argued that the Buddhist pursuit of emptiness, detachment, and openness can be emotionally sterile. Where does the heart exist if the *adept* is indifferent to all their desires and aversions? I love my family, so there's no way I can prevent attachments, worries, joys, and sufferings. Thus, I need to define the preferred objective/viewpoint to include something like "loving-kindness" as a fundamental component.

Years of meditation practice have convinced me of the mind's capacity to appreciate its fleeting awareness of self, others, and the rest of its constantly changing situation. Approaching each day with humble curiosity, I try to tenderly pay attention to whatever arises, knowing that some of it will be horrific, disgusting, and demoralizing.

Here is the proposed phrase I've been seeking for a viable, longer-term attitudinal goal: "Affectionate awareness." Of course, you need not adopt it dogmatically for any reason. See if it works; you may discover a better phrase that helps you on your way.

"Affectionate" encourages us to bring gentle kindness into our world and undercuts the critique that there is an impossible divide between loving-kindness and enhanced awareness. Let's have both! While the phrase is a bit Hallmarkey and verges on Madison Avenue sloganeering, you cannot easily wash it away with Holmes' "cynical acid" that uncovers selfish motives. "Affectionate" is not a purely selfish word; hope and kindness remain within its meaning as potential sources of sacrifice, generosity, and compassion.

Now, we can use a little pledge, set forth below, to help emerge from the doldrums, and not only struggle to survive but also make the most of our lives:

> *May I develop a dynamic viewpoint that enables me to create, evaluate, and maintain those worthwhile habits that will reinforce each other to create better odds for a longer life that is predominantly based upon "affectionate awareness."*

I have watched the mind for several decades, and I cannot verify whether there is an enduring decency that pervades my consciousness. I sure hope that is true, and my pure reason's imaginary powers are working hard to create a more benign Universe. Some might think that my growing belief in a closer link between reality and decency goes too far by blurring Hume's invaluable distinction between "is" and "ought." But, what if a deeply embedded sense of "ought" is already in the Universe that we encounter and often perceive? This is possibly a mystical question, but it may provide some hope and joy during these perilous times (and another reason to keep meditating).

While never totally convinced, I relied upon the faith that kindness and hope are not isolated phenomena. Who am I to reject that the Upanishad's theory of the "Self" (admired by the bleak Schopenhauer), which resides just below our ordinary awareness, may contain a range of moral traits and motives?

In addition, might the more detached, perceptual "Watcher" portion of our observing mind want to care for itself, knowing that it will disappear if its companion (the tangible being) should perish? In other words, a sense of greater awareness is more likely to last if this mode of consciousness takes care of its physical and mental condition and surroundings. If you have not encountered the concept of The Watcher before, our upcoming book, *Some Meditations for Those Who Have Lost Interest in Meditating*, will promote The Watcher's awareness as a central practice. Indeed, cultivating and empowering The Watcher—first by becoming more aware of its distinct perspective—may be a crucial early step in developing the deliberately obscure concept of *affectionate awareness*.

Chapter 11

Good Habits/Crossroads

January 18, 2023

A. GOOD HABITS

It is time to offer a cluster of "good habits" that not only may improve one's health but also the pursuit of affectionate awareness and other goals. These habits tend to reinforce each other, creating a virtuous circle that augments their benefits. Instead of a detailed, didactic series of newsletters about well-recognized good habits, we shall limit this description to those that seem to have helped me the most, and, hopefully, will be beneficial to others. In particular, we'll focus deeply on meditation and the ongoing battle to eliminate sugar from the diet.

Fortunately, the medical community is studying the relationships between habits and cancer outcomes. A recent article reviews studies of certain lifestyle habits and their apparent impacts on patients with glioblastoma.

Below are the habits that I follow closely, accompanied by core commitments. Note that some, but not all, of these coincide with those discussed in the medical article.

1. Diet. Absolutely no processed sugars and sweeteners. No alcohol. Limit carbohydrates to maintain weight at an appropriate BMI (Body Mass Index) level. CBD and eggs are great!

2. Exercise. Daily walking, dumbbells, balancing and stretching exercises, and so forth.

3. "Eastern Arts." Daily meditation and meditative practices (Tai Chi, Qi Gong, Yoga, etc.).

4. Mental Exercises. Reading a good book, writing, playing internet chess, engaging in interesting conversations, and so forth.

5. Friendship. Nurturing warm, accessible relationships with family, friends, neighbors, colleagues, and communities/neighborhoods. Don't forget your pets and favorite stuffed animals!

B. CROSSROADS: A NEW DIRECTION FOR THE NEWSLETTER

I haven't perfectly followed the habits listed above, but I believe they have strengthened my ability to fight cancer. Meditation, in particular, has proved to be a vital "Spiritual Swiss Army Knife," providing insight and relief from various afflictions. For decades, a dedicated practice has served me well during all kinds of situations. For example, my newest adversary is "chemo brain," a common side effect of cancer treatments, which makes me giddy and silly, distorting memory and perceptions along the way. It feels like being on a Ferris wheel that is pushing your mind into the air. So, to quote a classic meditator's recommendation, "Go sit on it."

I believe that regular, formal meditation strengthens the willpower to fight addictive bad habits and to adhere to the good habits. Greater self-discipline creates individual freedom by empowering one's will over abusive desires.

Rather than meandering miserably, while meticulously describing the latest variant of brain fog, I have decided to shift somewhat away from the diary-like narrative of *Cancer, Be Not Proud*. Otherwise, this newsletter could degrade into a tedious memoir entitled, *Fifty Shades of Brain Fog*.

Although we will continue to share important developments in my journey as part of the current series, we will embark soon on another series of newsletters, entitled, *Some Meditations for Those Who Have Lost Interest in Meditating*. We hope this endeavor will provide lasting benefits to interested readers, and a welcome respite from the grisly details of my latest treatment and drug effects (you certainly don't want to hear about my bouts of severe constipation!). Each installment in the meditation series will emerge from our overall umbrella, *Hope but No Expectations*, as did those in *Cancer, Be Not Proud*.

Chapter 12

Fear and Gratitude

March 26, 2023

Because of good news on the cancer front, your cancer war correspondent has veered, monkey-mind-like, off on a brief tangent from the meditation explorations to consider the emotional structure of our "moods." At our recent consult after last week's MRI and CT scans, the neuro oncologist said the status quo is still good. The blood clot is diminished, the single potential tumor is static, and there is no evidence of emerging problems in the brain or elsewhere.

The doctor's relaxed, enthusiastic body language suggested she is more hopeful and determined about my future. And the new chemo regime will be rotational, with two different drugs administered in sequence followed by six weeks without any chemo. No chemo for several weeks at a time sounds close to blissful! I can't say we have turned the corner (cautious optimism remains the emotional default), but it feels like a plausible possibility. Needless to say, this has improved my mood! Some friends say I look rejuvenated. The guy in my bathroom mirror looks less haggard.

We shall see the benefits of "getting in touch" with our emotions—even when they are disturbing—so that they can help us overcome myriad challenges. For example, because I received a positive doctor report and became less frightened, I was very tempted to relax some rules; the bright line against sugar came under attack and the little voice was more assertive and seductive. But when I considered a small indulgence, a jolt of fear was triggered, and my little voice quieted down.

"Mood" is a somewhat obscure word. It is Germanic, apparently a derivative of the German word for "mind." That broad conception can remind us that we should move beyond simple dichotomies when we study our "moods." As examples, when we consider the tragic/comic human masks of Grecian theater, the depression/mania of bipolar disorders, the "good mood/bad mood" dichotomy, it is easy to overlook the complexity of the "mood" that our mind carries with us. I like to envision my mood as the emotional stew that changes every day.

The trick, which may be enhanced by certain meditative practices that we'll discuss later, is to be aware of the ever-changing blend of ingredients. Currently, both fear and gratitude play far greater roles in my emotional stew than ever before.

As mentioned above, fear can be a motivator to remain committed to good habits. And gratitude motivates me to appreciate life more fully. I am eternally grateful for the friends, family members, neighbors, readers, and health-care providers, all of whom helped me get this far. I feel it is important to meditate on the outbreath with the word, "thanks," while contemplating both beautiful and everyday phenomena: the monarch butterfly dancing above the milkweed; the laundry bouncing noisily around in the dryer; the laughter of friends at a dinner table; the nuances of light that tickle the clouds; the crisp vegetables in a quinoa salad dropped off by a neighbor; and the hallucinogenic, colorful trunk of a rainbow eucalyptus tree.

Chapter 13

Diet and the Synergy of Good Habits

May 2, 2023

They call the changing sequence of drugs in chemotherapy a "rotation," but it frequently feels more like an ordeal. That old saying, "One Day at a Time," helps me through these drug-induced fluctuations and I feel more hopeful about my situation, which is far from the "all clear" prognosis. We've experienced a number of "highs," including a patio party to celebrate our supportive neighbors and friends, increased muscle strength due to disciplined exercise, and visits from relatives and friends who traveled far to get here. But there are also "lows" such as occasional dizziness, wobbliness, and extreme exhaustion. To continue the cancer war metaphor, it feels a lot like "battle fatigue." Oh, did I mention the vomiting and terrible rash from a recent round of antibiotics?

Right now, dwelling on such miseries only seems to make things worse. So, instead, I'll turn my attention to discuss more fully the diet that I'm following, which I hope others will find helpful. I firmly believe that my disciplined diet is prolonging my life and improving its quality. But, of course, I fully realize that it may not be a "cure-all."

There is a recent study concluding that deep-fried foods may contribute to anxiety and depression, in addition to excessive weight and other negative effects. So I have essentially eliminated all fried foods from my diet. Sugar is also a major contributor to obesity since it has significant calories and stimulates one's appetite. I have avoided refined sugars entirely for nearly eight months and have cut back dramatically on natural sweets in fruits and other sources. The anti-sugar regimen can be among the most demanding. And it is not enough to forego honey, maple syrup, coconut, and the myriad of artificial sweeteners. I have also eliminated all alcohol, not only because it converts easily to sugar but also because it diminishes willpower.

Both obesity and sugar have been shown to correlate somewhat with cancer, so they are a thing of the past for me. As a result, I have lost 35 pounds and feel much better about my weight and shape. My gut has taken a beating from the chemo and other treatments, so I have increased my water intake (hydrate, hydrate, hydrate!) and regularly eat natural probiotics such as sauerkraut, yoghurt, and Kefir.

A primary chemical-biological goal is to reduce inflammation, which contributes to chronic pain and cancer, according to various research. This consists of consuming anti-inflammatory foods and avoiding inflammatory foods. I follow this approach and believe it has reduced my own chronic pain and likelihood of injury due to overexertion. Harvard Medical School (HMS) has provided our foundation, with recommended lists for each.

Anti-inflammatory Food Sources:

- Leafy greens
- Beans
- Oranges
- Coffee
- Dark Chocolate

- Blueberries and other berries
- Cabbage (and other cruciferous vegetables)
- Eggplant
- Red grapes
- Colorful peppers
- Fatty fish (including salmon and tuna)
- CBD, ginger, turmeric

Foods to avoid (or at least limit) that can contribute to inflammation include meats (including chicken), sugars, deep-fried foods, processed meat, hot spices, and heavily processed carbohydrates. I am not a dietician, and certainly not a doctor, so I encourage you to read articles from authoritative sources. HMS has a *Special Health Report*, "Fighting Inflammation," which provides excellent information and is available for a low purchase price.

It may be important for certain people to take supplements. For example, vegans and vegetarians may need vitamin B-12. I have found a morning "daily egg" to be exceptionally helpful, providing protein, fat, B-12, appetite reduction, and greater energy. It's possible that a multivitamin offers somewhat of a hedge for addressing deficiencies. And, as I noted earlier, I take a daily dose of fermented food or drink that helps with my digestion, which has been battered from all the drugs.

Commitment and discipline are key perspectives to maintain, whether they pertain to diet, exercise, or meditation. I am gradually increasing my repetitions with dumbbells and resistance bands, and minutes on my Peloton bike. In addition, I am relearning Tai Chi after forgetting portions due to lack of practice following surgery. HMS recently published an article extolling the many benefits of Tai Chi. Others may want to take longer walks, swims, or workouts at the gym. Meditators can work on counting to higher numbers, practicing different word meditations, etc. May we all nurture our willpower as it protects us from dangerous, corrosive thoughts and desires while we also refrain the Will from becoming too bossy and judgmental.

If we try to accept life as it is, we also need to accept ourselves as we are. And so, as we explore the mind, we once again encounter a paradox: How can we accept ourselves while imposing many habits that disrupt our lives? No easy answer. This is a form of performance art—trying to balance determination, grace, judgment, and beauty.

Cautious optimism remains the best default. Still rejoicing in my relationships with this marvelous universe, I was delighted by a phrase recommended by a friend: "Open Heart/Open Mind."

Chapter 14

Another "Good Habit"

May 2, 2023

One advantage of developing an open meditation space that temporarily accepts whatever arises in the mind is that it gives the subconscious more opportunities to express itself via the intuitive process. Just a few days ago, I was slogging along in counting meditation when the following thought popped into my mind: creativity/aesthetic expression is another valuable habit to be cultivated. Some may disparage that claim as Monkey Mind business, but I believe it to be a burst of "creative intuition."

Indeed, one of meditation's benefits is that you have many more contacts with your subconscious and unconscious, starting with daydreaming. Renowned psychologist Carl Jung said aesthetics are our minds' lubricant and a manifestation of our subconscious. I don't want to stifle creativity with excessive demands, so my initial "identity-based requirement" is rather modest: write at least two newsletters per month. There, self-expression reaches a peak—a blend of discipline, intellect, memory, creativity, and imagination.

So, dear readers, I am grateful for your interest in my newsletter. A single letter checks many boxes for me: 1) intellectual stimulation; 2) creativity/ art; 3) enhancing affectionate relationships with my species; 4) trying to help others endure or overcome some of their suffering; and 5) continuing the exploration of the components of the mind.

It is somewhat embarrassing to admit that the pursuit of creativity had not been included in my initial list of important "good habits." Fortunately, habits can be modified by reason and experience. To practice creativity, you may want to keep a journal; try some doodling, painting or sketching; create a tune; or write a poem to a loved one. A more specific suggestion for experiencing creativity is to enjoy great artistic works such as David Lean & Alec Guinness' extraordinary trilogy: *Lawrence of Arabia, Doctor Zhivago,* and *The Bridge on the River Kwai*. Other recommendations include literary works by Jane Austen and Albert Camus. It's exhilarating and humbling to spend time with genius.

A few weeks ago, I had trouble getting out of my chair at a restaurant. An elderly man helped me. When I thanked him, he replied in an Eastern European accent: "We are all in the same world." This interaction touched me deeply. See? A little creative license enables us to feel our memories by writing about them.

Chapter 15

The Corner
May 21, 2023

Because there wasn't a brain scan before my recent appointment with the oncologist, we weren't expecting a significant prognosis about my condition. An appropriately cautious practitioner, the doctor usually left most of my future open-ended.

At the recent consult, I was exhausted by a wave of nasty mosquito bites that swelled and itched like crazy. During our conversation, I joked that we are pretty fortunate that our immediate concern had become bug bites, not just the life-threatening disease and agonizing side effects of treatments. She laughed. Towards the end of the session, I expressed a thought that was arguably overly optimistic. Throwing caution to the wind, I shared my growing sense that I have turned the corner. She brightly replied, "You *are* turning the corner."

Mimi and I celebrated for a day or two, but a slight wave of despondency emerged. Perhaps it was partially PTSD, but I foresaw how challenging it is to enter this new chapter. There are no guarantees, of course; it was a long walk to reach the corner and it will be a long walk to fully recover.

As my condition improves, I likely will become more observant of humanity's continuing death spiral. In addition, I will need even greater vigilance to prevent the hedonic principle from overwhelming the good habits that I believe have gotten me this far.

So, I invoked my "spiritual warrior" to keep fighting cancer currently, and to fulfill a prior commitment to stick with the good habits for at least 6-7 years after any significant prognosis, positive or negative. In other words, strict adherence until 2030.

You may have noticed that I included that hackneyed phrase, "spiritual warrior." For many years, I considered the notion an oxymoron; how can a "warrior" be "spiritual?" Thus, we will spend some time exploring my evolving understanding of that phrase. Alas, this inquiry drags us into the divisive domains of religion and politics, but I can't hide behind detachment forever. For example, I need to evaluate Josh Hawley's hypocritical drivel on masculinity and being a "warrior." Part of me would prefer to ignore such unpleasantries, but I might as well follow the intuitive processes that slipped onto this page.

Chapter 16

A New Chapter

May 30, 2023

Two developments support the hopeful prognosis that I have "turned the corner," possibly living for many years (assuming I comply with my good habits). First, my white blood cell (WBC) count, particularly the lymphocytes, recently increased after being dangerously low during April and early May due to the cumulative effects of chemo. Since I wasn't vaccinated recently for Covid due to my condition, I was particularly vulnerable and felt like I couldn't survive a serious infection. The low count is still of great concern, but for now I'm celebrating the uptick. Even my mosquito bites don't itch as much!!

Secondly, I am able to walk around the house most of the time without a walker or cane. I feel like a toddler who has gained basic autonomy. I can even prepare a simple breakfast, taking some pressure off my wonderful wife and caretaker.

These encouraging developments seem like the beginning of a new stage, requiring a new perspective. Previously, a single word or two could capture the situation. The first stage was largely about *shock* when I learned of my diagnosis of glioblastoma. The next stage in the hospital was all about *perseverance* and *war*. Later, while recovering at home, *fear* and *gratitude* were the primary motivators.

As I contemplate what to do next—what to do if I'm fortunate enough to live many more years—how should I proceed, even in terms of these newsletters? I needed to wait until my subconscious generated a strong signal, resonating throughout. When that occurred, the concept of compassion quickly took center stage. I may be cut short (like anyone else, and despite my healthy habits), but for the near term, focusing on compassion feels like the right approach.

So, what is compassion? How does it feel? Where does it fit in? How do we apply it? How do we distinguish between compassion for oneself and compassion for other beings?

The first step is to practice a few compassion meditations given by Pema Chödrön, who is superb at working with all sorts of emotions. Her meditation techniques have led me to recognize that one way I can act compassionately is by writing newsletters that might help to alleviate the suffering of others. During the early stages of my illness, I did not have the capacity to provide much compassion to others. Now that I am stronger, I can engage in these practices, which can sometimes be quite painful but can also lead to a greater appreciation of the value of compassion.

Chapter 17

Mixed News

June 30, 2023

Mimi and I recently adopted a slogan: "Mixed News is Good News." Almost every night, I encounter some insomnia, which provides plenty of time to exercise and meditate. My digestive tract remains dodgy, but there isn't any constipation. Once again, we are in yin-yang territory, requiring us to adapt to uncertainty, uneasiness, and insufficiency.

Today's major visit with our oncologist provided an intense example. The MRI on my enlarged prostate did not show any evidence of cancer! And the blood clotting in my brain has mostly dissipated, equally great news. But the more distressing part of the mix is that the brain MRI indicated a heightened intensity of white matter in a location that our doctors had been watching. As explained to us, this anomaly is likely due to one of two possible factors: residual effects of previous radiation, or an active tumor. An upcoming PET scan should reveal which one it is. If there is tumor growth, it's quite possible I will have additional radiation treatment, which, hopefully, will destroy the tumor without causing many side effects. Fortunately, no additional tumors have appeared elsewhere.

In any case, I will soon begin a new chemo regimen. Previous rounds of Temodar and CCNU (Lomustine) likely were responsible for driving down the lymphocyte count in my white blood cells, weakening my immune system and making me very vulnerable to Covid and other infectious diseases. A certain type of pneumonia is a serious threat, and I now take Pentamidine (inhalation) treatments that hopefully will protect me.

So, unfortunately, my weak immune system is prohibiting me from most social interactions, while the intense heat and mosquitoes are keeping me mostly indoors (except for trips to medical appointments). And now, it's known that some mosquitoes are carrying malaria. So, it looks like I'll be a recluse for a while.

The good habits of healthy diet, daily exercise, consistent meditation, writing the newsletter, and human interactions (albeit limited) provide ways to weather this murky situation. Also, we can still celebrate the fading away of the prostate problem and blood clot. Mixed is good. Obviously, psychological deterioration could escalate. However, adhering to good habits increases willpower, and my Will seeks to live with increased vigor.

By adopting the "Watcher" perspective from meditation practices, I can gaze at this gloomy scene, alternating between sadness, fear and gratitude—and contemplate my continuing ability to see, hear, think and feel. As Calvin and Hobbes observed, "It is a Magical World."

A friend recently observed that fighting cancer is an up and down affair. So is life.

Thanks to all of you for helping me make it through a particularly harrowing period since my diagnosis. We are still in the fight of a lifetime. Our mixed mental arts may carry us a long way.

Chapter 18

War and Pride

August 28, 2023

Today, August 28, 2023, is the one-year anniversary of our trip to the Tampa General Emergency Department and my jarring transition into an ailing patient needing to fight a particularly aggressive brain cancer, glioblastoma. My initial goal was to live for at least another year. Hence, it is an appropriate time to celebrate this annual milestone and wrap it up as the concluding chapter for the soon-to-be-published book, *Cancer, Be Not Proud*, which contains newsletters of the same title on Substack, https://hopebutnoexpectations.substack.com/

While there has been much suffering, we shall consider how the cancer experience improved my life in ways that far exceeded earlier hopes and expectations. The list could go on and on: eating buttered popcorn with a neighbor while watching baseball; laughing with my masseuse at our imagined antics of a stuffed animal, Curious George, an avatar we purchased to acknowledge the "Monkey Mind;" watching a night heron pick through the grass before marching down our street for a second course; taking Peloton bike rides along some of the world's most beautiful trails;

delighting in the company of friends and neighbors on our front porch; and feeling the joy of being able to type again with only minimal typos.

Above all, my love and respect for my wife and primary caretaker, Mimi, has soared. They weren't kidding about the "in sickness and in health" wedding vow. For the past year, we have called our home "Fort Willord," a cheerful blend of our surnames, Wilson and Lord. Like most decent people, we spent many demanding years trying to help our family members and community. Right now, we enjoy sitting on a nearby park bench to appreciate the daily sunrise. We embrace the beauty of pelicans gliding just above a pastel Tampa Bay, reflecting the sunrise, a scene that also reflects the existential beauty of our refusal to capitulate to difficult or negative forces.

So many family members, friends, neighbors, and others have provided a scrumptious blend of emotional support, humor, and home-cooked meals. These unsolicited visits and gifts are the epitome of compassionate generosity. Recently, our two children have found more satisfying work; I am proud of their contributions to society and unwillingness to submit to the more corrosive aspects of our often-decadent culture. Their laughter-filled enthusiasm last Thanksgiving helped me turn the corner; additional visits have replenished the soul.

Writing this newsletter has been particularly rewarding and gratifying, alleviating a gnawing disappointment caused by the legal academy's lack of interest in my scholarship. So, the fulsome appreciation from fellow writers and other readers—including many who also are battling the vicissitudes of old age, sickness, and death—has been very validating and fulfilling.

As far as I can tell, developing and maintaining the cluster of good habits that I recommended as a chemistry experiment may have really worked! For instance, we recently heard results of a very favorable PET scan. But this conflict is far from over. Perhaps others will benefit from taking a similar path, flourishing from the synergistic effects of sticking with multiple habits. I hope to carry the discipline, energy, and focus into the future as a "cancer survivor."

Were cancer and death to enter our home as the least invited guests of all time, I would laugh, saying, "See what you have done? You are not so all-powerful after all. We've got way more pride than you two goons will ever have."

So how should we take any such transformative experiences into our troubled world? Let's escape from American capitalism's systemic atomization and accompanying alienation to cheerfully acknowledge how interdependent and intertwined we are.

Acknowledgements

This book would not have been written without the extraordinary caretaking and editing by my wife, Mimi Lord. She has been a lifelong writer in her own right, but more lucid and thorough than her husband.

Our children Lee and Nathan have brought us tremendous joy; they have helped me maintain hope and a growing determination to continue the good fight. We are deeply grateful also to our brothers and their spouses, extended families, numerous friends, and our healthcare providers at Tampa General Hospital—particularly our neuro and radiation oncologists, Dr. Tulika Ranjan and Dr. Brian Collins, respectively.

We also want to thank *Stacy Higgins*, a marketing designer, who formatted the content into this lovely book and navigated the publication process for us.

The yin/yang infinity symbol represents a concept in ancient Chinese philosophy where opposite forces are shown as interconnected and counterbalancing.

The image on the front cover is titled, "Under the Great Wave off Kanagawa." It is a woodblock print by the renowned Japanese artist, Katsushika Hokusai, created in 1830-31. I chose it as a visual metaphor for the struggle against cancer: "one wave at a time."

The photo on the back cover, taken by Mimi at Tampa Bay, captures a calmer sense of water and waves, which has provided us with great comfort. Nearly every morning, we make our short trek to watch a beautiful sunrise over the water.

This book, *Cancer Be Not Proud*, is one of a series of Jim's Newsletters under the umbrella title, *Hope But No Expectations*. You may read all his newsletters and subscribe to receive future ones at *https://hopebutnoexpectations.substack.com/*.

Photo by Alicia Reyes

Jim, Mimi and their beloved dog, Nina, enjoying one of many afternoons at The North Carolina Arboretum in the fall of 2021.